FROM **EGG** TO
CHICKEN

by Robin Nelson

Lerner Publications Company / Minneapolis

Lerner Publications Company
A division of Lerner Publishing Group
241 First Avenue North
Minneapolis, MN 55401 U.S.A.

Website address: www.lernerbooks.com

Library of Congress Cataloging-in-Publication Data

Nelson, Robin, 1971–
    From egg to chicken / by Robin Nelson.
      p.   cm. — (Start to finish)
    Contents: A mother chicken lays eggs.—The hen sits on
the eggs.—A baby chicken grows.—The baby chicken
cracks the shell.—The baby chicken leaves its shell.—
Feathers keep the chick warm.—The chick finds food.—
The chick grows.—Hello Chicken!
    ISBN: 0–8225–4662–0 (lib. bdg. : alk. paper)
    1. Chicks—Juvenile literature. 2. Chickens—Juvenile
literature. [1. Chickens. 2. Animals—Infancy.] I. Title.
II. Start to finish (Minneapolis, Minn.)
SF498.4 .N45 2003
636.5—dc21   2002009861

Manufactured in the United States of America
2 3 4 5 6 7 – DP – 09 08 07 06 05 04

The photographs in this book appear courtesy of:
© Superstock, cover; © Julie Habel/Corbis, pp. 1
(both), 5; © Inga Spence/Visuals Unlimited, p. 3;
© Lynn M. Stone, p. 7; © Robert Pickett/Corbis,
pp. 9, 13; © David Spindel/Superstock, p. 11;
© William J. Webber/Visuals Unlimited, pp. 15, 19;
Ken Hammond/USDA, p. 17; © Trinity Muller/
Independent Picture Service, p. 21; © Norva Behling,
p. 23.

Table of Contents

Cluck, cluck!

How does a chicken grow?

A mother chicken lays eggs.

A female chicken is called a **hen**. A hen lays many eggs. Inside each egg is a baby chicken.

The hen sits on the eggs.

The hen sits on her eggs. She keeps the eggs warm to help her babies grow.

A baby chicken grows.

A chicken begins as a small spot on an egg **yolk**. The yolk is the yellow part of an egg. The baby gets food from the yolk. Food helps the baby grow and grow.

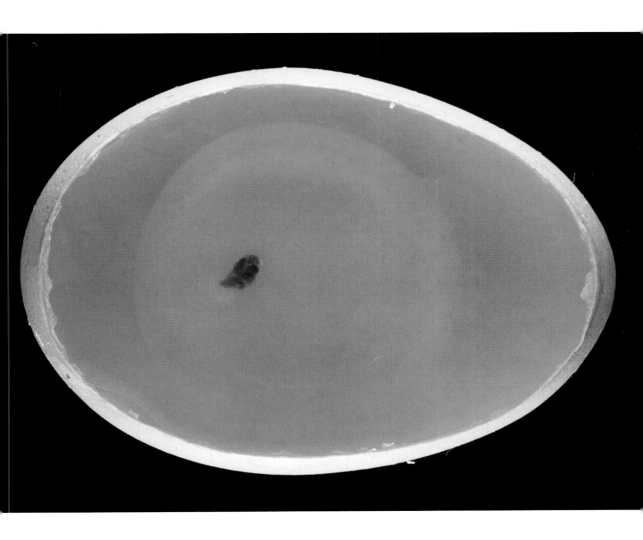

9

The baby chicken cracks the shell.

The hard part of a chicken's mouth is called a **beak**. A baby chicken has an **egg tooth** on its beak. The baby grows until it is ready to leave the egg. Then it cracks its shell with its egg tooth.

The baby chicken leaves its shell.

The shell breaks open. The baby chicken leaves the shell. Now it is called a **chick**.

The chick stays close to the hen.

The chick is weak and wet. It snuggles under its mother to keep warm. The chick dries after a few hours.

Feathers keep the chick warm.

The chick is covered with soft, fluffy feathers called **down**. Down keeps the chick warm.

The chick finds food.

The chick pecks the ground to look for food. It eats insects and seeds.

The chick grows.

The chick grows for a few weeks. The chick's down begins to fall out. Adult feathers grow. Adult feathers are not as soft and fluffy as down.

Hello, chicken!

The chick has grown up. Now it
is a chicken.

Glossary

beak (BEEK): the hard part of a chicken's mouth

chick (CHIHK): a young chicken

down (DOWN): soft, fluffy feathers

egg tooth (EHG TOOTH): a tooth used to break a shell

hen (HEHN): a female chicken

yolk (YOHK): the yellow part of an egg

Index